SENT!

A HANDBOOK FOR EFFECTIVE EVANGELISM

Andrew Owen

REAPERS TRUST

Reapers Trust ®

First published by Harvestime as "Go and Evangelise"
First printed June 1992
Revised May 2000

ISBN 0 9524643 2 2

Cover Design:
Verve Creative, Glasgow G60 5JU

Typeset in the United Kingdom by:
Summit Media & Print Ltd, Glasgow G60 5JU

This study is dedicated to those who have pioneered with me on many occasions. Those who, when we were only a handful, believed God could use us to grow something significant: these are the true Bravehearts. May God give us many more pioneers like them.

Andrew Owen

Contents

Unless otherwise stated, scripture quotations are taken from the New International Version.

Other versions referred to in this series Include the New American Standard Bible (NASB), the Revised Authorised Version (RAV) and the Amplified Bible (Amp).

LESSON 1

Called to the Frontline

"All the planning of men may change the world and still leave it as it is."
William Barclay

We live in an age of incredible mass communication. It is the age of satellites, digital broadcasting, web surfing and e-commerce. All over the world this electronic wizardry relays billions of pieces of information. 'Narrow-casting' is a newly-coined term expressing the growing markets in specialised programme making, satisfying the interests of ethnic and other special interest groups .

Yet despite this technological advance:

- One in three marriages ends in divorce.
- Cardboard cities are still emerging filled with hurting children who have run away from broken homes.
- Many charities are inundated with calls from desperately lonely people.
- Peace talks fail as nations refuse to come to the conference table.
- Economic collapse leaves the children of the so-called superpower countries begging for bread.

It is clear that, while man has the ability to circulate information, **he has failed to impart life-giving truth**. Humanistic values have caused this world to treat man as merely a body with a brain. Such values have failed to recognise him as a person created in the image and likeness of God, giving no thought for his soul.

We may have a wealth of material things, but, as Jesus said, “A man’s life does not consist in the abundance of his possessions.” See (Luke 12:15.) Life cannot be collected; it must be found and lived.
Man's first need is spiritual. Until that need is met, the best that society can do is to put sticking plasters on decaying corpses.

John writes and tells us that healthy lives are directly connected to healthy souls!

> *‘Dear friend, I pray that you may enjoy good health and that all may go well with you, even as your soul is getting along well.’*
>
> **3 John:2**

We, however, have been entrusted with the answer.

1. Called to Go

“To be hatched, matched and dispatched.” That was how one man on the street answered when questioned about the role of the church in the community. He saw the church as only adding the frills to a predetermined sequence of events - birth, marriage and death. The possibility that the church might have the answer to life's questions had never even entered his head.

Christians, likewise, so often see the church as remote from the world around them. They often view it as a safe haven from the unpleasant world. They appear interested only in the height of praise or the depth of the preached word. Their first consideration is whether or not the church is meeting their own needs.

Many other Christians will attend revival prayer meetings or take 30 day fasts asking God to move - but maybe, just maybe, he’s waiting for us!

The church was not brought to birth by God for defensive purposes; it was initiated by him for advance:

> *'Go into all the world and preach the good news to all creation.'*
> **Mark 16:15**

While people and nations seek better ways to manage their economies, God seeks people. His purposes are achieved by people - people like you and me who are to be his secret weapon, his frontline troops:

> *'His intent was that now through the church, the manifold wisdom of God should be made known to the rulers and authorities in the heavenly realms'.*
> **Ephesians 3:10**

God can do extraordinary things through ordinary people!

2. A Covenant Obligation

God wants to be closely bound to his people. Covenant, one of the major themes of Scripture, could be defined as a contract or agreement that makes this possible. God's dealings with people like Adam, Noah and David always had the elements of a covenant relationship. A covenant relationship is always hallmarked by:

- It is initiated by God.
- It has a covenantal mandate - clear terms to be fulfilled by each party. In Adam's case, God said, *'Fill the earth and subdue it.'* Genesis 1:28.
- God gives resource to accomplish the task. With Adam, food was provided to enable him to work. Genesis 1:29 (and of course a partner!)

In other words GOD ALWAYS MAKES PROVISION FOR THE VISION. When God made a covenant with the nation of Israel, he gave them the mandate to be a light to all nations. Contrary to their belief, God did not have a most favoured nation clause in his contract; his eye and heart were always towards the whole world:

> *'I will make you a light for the Gentiles, that you may bring my salvation to the ends of the earth.'*
>
> **Isaiah 49:6**

Israel violated this covenant by their selfish, insular ways. Yet when we consider the New Covenant, in which we have a part, we find that Jesus makes this same mandate:

> *'Go and make disciples of all nations, baptising them in the name of the Father and of the Son and of the Holy Spirit, and teaching them to obey everything I have commanded you. And surely I am with you always, to the very end of the age.'*
>
> **Matthew 28:19-20**

Evangelism is included in the mandate of the New Covenant.

God takes covenant very seriously, even ratifying it in blood. He declares himself to be a covenant-keeping God (see, for example, Leviticus 26:9). This adds greater urgency to our task of evangelism - **It is required covenantally.**

3. All Included

We are a people who have a purpose. Evangelism is not one of those areas a Christian can choose. It is a heavenly call placed upon him. Don't choose as optional what God considers essential!

In many churches, seminars are presented on important issues for those who feel called to a certain task. But we are all called to be witnesses!

> *'You are a people, a royal priesthood a holy nation, a people belonging to God that you may declare the praises of him who called you out of darkness into his wonderful light.'*
>
> **1 Peter 2:9**

The word 'declare' is the Greek verb *exangello*. It emphasises the need to "fully proclaim" or "publish completely". Early in my Christian life, older men of God reminded me, 'You're saved to serve.' The principle of the verse is that we have become someone to do something.

4. Freedom in Christ

> *'It is for freedom that Christ has set us free. Stand firm, then, and do not let yourselves be burdened again by a yoke of slavery.'*
>
> **Galatians 5:1**

When you become a Christian, the power that once held you is broken, and you are set free. God's idea of freedom is not giving you the liberty to do what you want, but the power to do what you ought!

5. Doing the work of an Evangelist

The noun 'evangelist' (Greek *euangelistes*) appears only three times in the New Testament

- *'We stayed at the house of Philip the evangelist' (Acts 21:8).*
- *'It was he who gave... some to be evangelists' (Epheslans 4: 11).*
- *'Do the work of an evangelist' (2 Timothy 4:5).*

Some scholars claim that the original Greek term 'evangelist' was applied not to a Christian office but to a slave whose assignment was to serve alongside an army general. If their side won, his task was to run with the news of his general's victory. Mothers, daughters and wives would be worrying about the outcome of the battle, but when they saw the evangelist coming, they knew they had won!

The coming of the evangelist always preceded the coming of the victor; his news prepared the people for the victory celebrations - it's party time. We are not necessarily called to be eloquent or absolutely correct in our presentation of the gospel. We are simply to tell of the victory that has been won. Often the Greek evangelist would have been too excited to proclaim with accurate grammar the exact events of battle, but his joy, enthusiasm and great excitement said it all! Sometimes, it's not what you say but how you say it that has the greatest impact.

To evangelise is to run with the good news of victory. It is to carry the message of faith, hope, promise and freedom. We are not passport providers for the afterlife, but heralds of a kingdom coming with power and majesty:

> *'How beautiful on the mountains are the feet of those who bring good news, who proclaim peace, who bring good tidings, who proclaim salvation, who say to Zion, "Your God reigns!"'*
>
> **Isaiah 52:7**

The Concise Oxford Dictionary defines communication as 'the act of imparting', 'the information communicated' or 'a means of connecting different places, such as a door, passage, road or railway'. We are the connection between life and death for many; we are the link in the chain that makes the best possible introduction. We can win people to ourselves and introduce them to our best friend, Jesus.

The coming of the Greek evangelist preceded the coming of his general, preparing the people for his arrival. There is an implication in Scripture that a rapid rise in world-wide evangelism and a powerful outpouring of the Spirit to empower the church will precede the second coming of Jesus:

> *"In the last days", God says, "I will pour out my Spirit on all people."*
>
> **Acts 2:17**

6. Life Communicators

While the term for evangelist only appears three times in the New Testament, the Greek verb *euangelizo*, which means 'to announce good news', occurs fifty two times. Most of the proclamation, it would appear, was done other than by the evangelist:

a. God

The first person mentioned as having proclaimed the good news was God himself when he preached to the heathen idolater, Abram. That encounter changed the man's name, his life and the world:

> *'The Scripture foresaw that God would justify the Gentiles by faith, and announced the gospel in advance to Abraham.'*
>
> **Galatians 3:8**

Could this be the record of the first evangelistic crusade? God the evangelist preaching at a meeting when only one turned up? But what a response!

God is not a recluse; he communicates. He communicated an undying love for a dying world. It has been said, "You can only see eye to eye when you are standing face to face." God came and stood face to face with the human race:

> *'In the past God spoke to our forefathers through the prophets at many times and in various ways, but in these last days he has spoken to us by his son whom he has appointed heir of all things, and through whom he made the universe.'*
>
> **Hebrews 1:1-2**

When Jesus came, guesswork about God ended. No longer were we to wonder what he was like, what he required or what he offered. Jesus made it all clear. Sometimes we get discouraged with low attendance at our evangelistic events. At God's first recorded encounter, there was only one person present, but that one really mattered.

b. Jesus

Jesus was sent, but he also proclaimed. He came 'to seek and to save what was lost.' Luke 19:10

> *'One day as he (Jesus) was teaching the people in the temple courts and preaching the gospel, the chief priests and the teachers of the law, together with the elders, came up to him.'*
>
> ***Luke 20:1***

Jesus is the best example of an evangelist. At every turn he looked for those to whom he might proclaim the good news. In tiredness and difficulty he consistently reached out. Even on the cross, his last act was to bring good news to the dying thief at his side.

c. Ordinary Christians

God always turns the devil's ills to his own advantage. When persecution came to those early Christians, rather than dying they grew:

> *'Those who had been scattered preached the word wherever they went.'*
>
> **Acts 8:4**

d. Evangelists

> *'Philip went down to a city in Samaria and proclaimed the Christ there.'*
>
> **Acts 8:5**

e. Apostles

> *'Paul was preaching the good news about Jesus and the resurrection.'*
>
> **Acts 17:18**

It is clear that evangelism was a major preoccupation for all of them. The result was that ever-increasing circles of influence impacted the world. It was just as Jesus had said - Jerusalem, Judea, Samaria, the ends of the earth (see Acts 1:8).

7. God and Sons Unlimited

We have seen that most of the evangelism in the early church was done by most of the people. It was not considered the expert's job. Evangelistic campaigns with an invited evangelist were alien to those first-century believers. God has also called us to participate in the family business, to become paid-up shareholders and to expect a return on our investment.

a. Great expectations

For many, evangelism has become a chore laid on them, from which they expect little result. After all, they are shy, and their past moves into enemy territory have led only to embarrassment and have damaged already vulnerable egos. Yet Jesus promised much more:

> *'You did not choose me, but I chose you and appointed you to go and bear fruit - fruit that will last. Then the Father will give you whatever you ask in my name.'*
>
> **John 15:16**

If you are locked up by shyness - let God unlock you!

b. Delivered from the curse

Some Christians will be shocked when they arrive in heaven, for it will not be the rest-home they imagined, where the 'curse' of work will be removed. They believe work of any kind was the outcome of the fall, yet Jesus points out:

> *'My Father is always at his work to this very day and I, too, am working.'*
>
> **John 5:17**

Work was not the result of the fall; barrenness and fruitlessness were. God said to Adam:

> *'Cursed is the ground because of you; through painful toil you will eat of it all the days of your life.'*
>
> **Genesis 3:17**

Now, however, that curse has been removed:

> *'Christ redeemed us from the curse of the law by becoming a curse for us.'*
>
> **Galatians 3:13**

While we still await creation's redemption, as children of God we can expect that, when we are aligned to his will, what we do will succeed:

> *'O Lord, save us; O Lord, grant us success. Blessed is he who comes in the name of the Lord.'*
>
> **Psalm 118:25-26**

c. Theatre of operations

During the 90's The Gulf War took place. At this point a new phrase found its way into our vocabulary - 'theatre of operations'. It referred to the specific area within which the assault was taking place. From God's viewpoint, the whole world is his theatre of operation. For you and me it is that community within which we have been strategically placed by God. It's your office, your home, your school. As someone once said "the ends of the earth start at your end."

With right thinking I will fulfil my covenant obligation, expecting not frustration but success. Somewhere someone's life is going to change for the better because of their encounter with me.

> *'Therefore prepare your minds for action.'*
>
> **1 Peter 1:13**

Someone once said that we the church should ask ourselves "what is our business?" and then further ask "How is business?"

With God we make it a success.
"I will go anywhere, as long as it is forward." David Livingstone

Lesson 1

Called to the Frontline

True or False

1. T F The purpose of the church is to provide a safe haven for Christians.
2. T F Evangelism is required by God covenantally.
3. T F Evangelism is a specialised ministry for those who are called to it.
4. T F I can choose whether to participate in evangelism.
5. T F The word 'declare' in 1 Peter 2:9 means to fully proclaim and publish completely.
6. T F I can expect to see results through my witnessing.
7. T F The first person mentioned as proclaiming the good news was God himself.
8. T F Work was the result of the fall.
9. T F The way I think determines the way I live.

Group Discussion

I. What does covenant mean to each member of the group? How does this affect our attitude towards the covenantal mandate?

2. What does freedom in Christ mean to us?

Personal Assignment

1. Make a study of Psalm 1. How should you live in order to expect prosperity in all you do?
2. Consider evangelism in the light of 1 John 3:8. What implication does that have on the people you know?

True or False

1.F 2.T 3.F 4.F 5.T 6.T 7.T 8.F 9.T

LESSON 2

Equipped for the Task

'If you don't like what you're reaping, change what you're sowing.'
Andrew Owen

1. The Right Tools for the Job

> *'You will receive power when the Holy Spirit comes on you; and you will be my witnesses in Jerusalem, and in all Judea and Samaria, and to the ends of the earth.'*
>
> **Acts 1:8**

The mandate of the New Covenant is to make disciples. But as with all other covenants, God not only instructs us to do something, but provides the means by which we can do it. He doesn't ask us to do something and then abandon us to our own efforts. He always provides provision for the vision.

A tradesman would be foolish to attempt to do a skilful job without using the proper tools. The key tool to successful evangelism, no matter what it's format, is the Holy Spirit. We are promised power to be witnesses. This 'power' is the Greek word *dunamis*. It speaks of power in action, not just latent power. It is something that outworks. From it we get our English word 'dynamite'. *Dunamis* has the ability to break open, pull down and cut away. It changes things.

2. Co-workers

> *'Jesus said, "with man this is impossible but with God all things are possible."'*
>
> **Matthew 19:26**

Often Christians quote this verse in some difficult situation, or when an answer to prayer is required. If it is read in its context, it is clear that Jesus was speaking about people being born again into God's kingdom. His emphasis was that what we would consider naturally impossible becomes possible in God's realm. Have you perhaps, misread this verse? It doesn't say, '**For** God all things are possible'. We know everything is possible for God. But it says, '**with** God'. The word 'with' is the Greek word *para*, which means 'alongside'. Suddenly it isn't us on our own, or God doing it all; it is us alongside him. It brings Almighty God into the here and now. It is a partnership that makes everything possible.

> *'Since we live by the Spirit, let us keep in step with the spirit.'*
> **Galatians 5:25**

Too mant people are working 'for' God. God doesn't want anyone to work '**for**' him. He wants people to work '**with**' him!

3. Coached Into Success

> *'The Counsellor, the Holy Spirit, whom the Father will send in my name, will teach you all things and will remind you of everything I have said to you.'* **John 14:26**

The name given by Jesus to the Holy Spirit is 'Comforter' or 'Counsellor'. It is the Greek word *parakletos* and means 'called alongside to give aid'. Often we interpret 'Comforter' simply as someone who cheers us up when we are down or are having a difficult time. But Jesus saw the Holy Spirit as an aid, a help, an inspirer and a teacher. Like an athletics coach, the Spirit helps us run the race with the best possible results. Effective evangelism comes mostly, not from technique, but from togetherness, walking with the Holy Spirit.

4. The Pincer Movement

God not only has an aim in sight - to make himself famous in the whole earth - but also has a strategy for how to get there. We need to be aware of the

Holy Spirit's strategy so that we can take advantage of it and co-operate with him. It's a pincer movement in that he works in two directions, capturing the person in the middle:

a. In the world

> *'When he comes he will convict the world of guilt in regard to sin and righteousness and judgement.'*
>
> **John 16:8**

It is impossible to be born again without first being convicted by the Holy Spirit of the need of a Saviour. Once that has been achieved, he points us in the direction of Christ. He is at work among our neighbours, friends and acquaintances. We would do well to listen to his footsteps and follow his lead. We don't have a monopoly on the Holy Spirit - he is a free agent and goes where he pleases.

Not everyone is open to the gospel. Before an encounter with the Father, a person must come through the Son. The Spirit shows him or her the way. Jesus said:

> *'All that belongs to the Father is mine. That is why I said the Spirit will take from what is mine and make it known to you.'*
>
> **John 16:15**

People must first know the convicting of the Holy Spirit before they can respond. This can happen as we speak to them, or it can be the result of several encounters with God's Word. Either way, it cannot be done without the Holy Spirit

Locked in – but locked out

So often Christians lock into some close relative or neighbour who has no flicker of interest in the gospel. They become their target; they must see this person come through to salvation. They then close all other doors, feeling that if they fail here, they will fail everywhere.

Their greatest failure, however, is not to see that lady at the school gate who is desperately searching, or that shopper who longs for the answers to life. Jesus spent his time looking for those who were open.

Let's be creative!

> *'The next day Jesus decided to leave for Galilee. Finding Philip, he said to him, "Follow me."'*
>
> **John 1:43**

b. In us

> *'Do not get drunk on wine, which leads to debauchery. Instead, be (continually) filled with the Spirit.'*
>
> **Ephesians 5:18**

The person who successfully wins others is the person who knows how to walk with the Holy Spirit. Once that person has received the Holy Spirit's empowering, God has the ability to make divine connections. God can do amazing things through ordinary people.

5. Catching the Coach

> *'May the grace of the Lord Jesus Christ, and the love of God, and the fellowship of the Holy Spirit be with you all.'*
>
> **2 Corinthians 13:14**

If the key to success is the Holy Spirit, we need to know how to stay alongside him. Here are some pointers:

a. An initial infilling

> *'Repent and be baptised, every one of you, in the name of Jesus Christ for the forgiveness of your sins. And you will receive the gift of the Holy Spirit. The promise is for you and your children and for all who are far off - for all whom the Lord our God will call.'*
>
> **Acts 2:38-39**

This encounter of the baptism in the Holy Spirit changed the already believing disciples from fearful fugitives into bold proclaimers. Jesus' instruction to his disciples was that they were not to move until they had been equipped with the Holy Spirit. We would be foolish to try to move without him.

b. Speak to him as a friend

Many Christians mistakenly believe that it is wrong to pray to or speak with the Holy Spirit. While his function is to point us towards Christ, who in turn introduces us to the Father, he is nevertheless God Almighty. As such, he speaks, hears and can be grieved.

You would not enjoy fellowship with a close friend without conversation, so it is with God the Holy Spirit. Fellowship is a two-way thing. You share your heart and invite guidance in all areas of your life.

c. Live with a Clear Conscience

Conscience can be defined as a 'knowing within'. Feelings are the voice of your body, reason is the voice of the mind and the conscience is the voice of the Spirit. An impaired conscience leads to an ineffective life. You must guard your conscience and not offend it, treating it with the utmost respect. Your conscience can be numbed by constant, unrepentant sin.

For many people, however, sin is not the issue. They lack the right kind of co-knowledge: and don't understand what God has done for them:

> *'This... is how we know that we belong to the truth, and how we set our hearts at rest in his presence whenever our hearts condemn us. For God is greater than our hearts and he knows everything.'*
>
> **1 John 3:19-20**

We are called to the frontline of evangelism. We need to ensure that when conscience is considered, we don't find wrong motivations propelling our hearts and lives into action.

> *'Above all else, guard your heart, for it is the wellspring of life.'*
>
> **Proverbs 4:23**

Our sharing of our faith should not be:

I. *To earn God's favour*

Effective evangelism comes from close communion with the Spirit, and that can come only from knowing that you are accepted:

> *'Let us . . . . approach the throne of grace with confidence so that we may receive mercy and find grace to help us in our time of need.'*
>
> **Hebrews 4:16**

2. *Out of a sense of guilt*

Sometimes evangelism can be motivated out of a sense that it needs to be done. This can lead to an unannounced assault on a stranger. It can also make people feel that the sooner they get it over with the better. Such motivation is unbelief, and the result is always ineffective.

3. *In an effort to repay God*

With deep gratitude to God, we can find ourselves motivated by wanting to give him something in return. Many Christians are out on a limb in their service to God. Yet we can never repay him. We must instead abandon ourselves to his loving care, looking to become living sacrifices, available for him to use at his discretion. We don't work *for* God; we work *with* him.

> *'I urge you, brothers in view of God's mercy, to offer your bodies as living sacrifices, holy and pleasing to God - this is your spiritual act of worship.'*
>
> **Romans 12:1**

4. *Motivated by anything other than love*

> *'Love is patient, love is kind. It does not envy, it does not boast, it is not proud. It is not rude, it is not self seeking, it is not easily angered, it keeps no record of wrongs. Love does not delight in evil but rejoices with the truth. It always protects, always trusts, always hopes, always perseveres.'*
>
> **1 Corinthians 13:4-7**

God's motivation towards us is love. Love ought to be our motivation towards the world. Often we are too quick to see people as statistics, failing to see that each of them has a name and a story to tell. It is our responsibility to do good to all people, irrespective of the response, results or returns that we get (see Galatians 6.10).

People followed Jesus for all the wrong reasons – food, miracles or healings. Yet even though he knew many would never stay with him, he did good to all people. He encourages us to be motivated in that same way:

> *'Jesus Christ... gave himself for us to redeem us from all wickedness and to purify for himself a people that are his very own, eager to do what is good.'*
>
> **Titus 2:13-14**

Check that your desire to do good doesn't change when it is a stranger who is passing by, someone you will never see again. Are you motivated by wanting something in return - or by genuine love?

> *'Christ's love compels us because we are convinced that one died for all'.*
>
> **2 Corinthians 5:14**

We cannot become what we need to be by remaining what we are.

6. Faith is Not Enough

Often evangelism starts enthusiastically with strong expectancy and 'faith' to see things happen, But when none of your friends accepts your invitation, your 'faith' wanes. Maybe you decide to join the door-visitation team. It is cold and wet, and every response is negative. Your 'faith' now dies.

It is not having faith that matters; it is the kind of faith you have:

> *'We do not want you to become lazy, but to imitate those who through faith and patience inherit what has been promised.'*
>
> **Hebrews 6:12**

As the famous missionary and evangelist Hudson Taylor once said, 'There are three phases in most great tasks undertaken:
1. Impossible; 2. Difficult; 3. Done!

You would think it foolish of the hardworking farmer to dig up seed he had only sown the day before, simply because the growth was not yet evident; yet Christians do that all the time with God's promises. If there are no instant results, they throw away the promises rather than persevere.

Webster's Dictionary defines 'persevere' as 'to continue in some effort, course of action, in spite of difficulty, opposition.'

That great wartime hero, Winston Churchill, to whom the British nation is indebted, said, **'I do not intend to take that cowardly course, but, on the contrary, to stand at my post and persevere in accordance with my duty as I see it'** For him, the cowardly course was to compromise with the enemy, ignore the plight of other nations and settle for the line of least resistance. He didn't take that course, however, and through much discouragement, he persevered on to success.

7. Praying Effectively

When it comes to prayer for people to be born again, many Christians are all at sea. Their praying tends to be unreal optimism.

What is the right way to pray? Is it right simply to pray for thousands to be saved? Can we expect God to save our unsaved family members when their wills are resisting Christ's lordship? We know God answers prayer. How, then, should we pray? Here are some clear examples:

a. Pray for more workers

> *'The harvest is plentiful, but the workers are few. Ask the Lord of the harvest, therefore, to send out workers into his harvest field.'*
>
> **Luke 10:2**

b. Pray for boldness

Nowhere do you find the Christians of the early church praying for power to be witnesses. They knew that God had given them all that was required. But we do find them praying for boldness:

> *'Now Lord, consider their threats and enable your servants to speak your word with great boldness.'*
>
> **Acts 4:29**

God is the source of your power and supply. Pray for boldness to move out from this deposit. The Holy Spirit can change peoples temperament. He can change your shyness and timidity into confidence and strength.

c. Pray for God's confirmation and ownership

> *'Stretch out your hand to heal and perform miraculous signs and wonders through the name of your holy servant Jesus.'*
>
> **Acts 4:30**

> *'The disciples went out and preached everywhere and the Lord*

worked with them and confirmed his word by the signs that accompanied it.'

Mark 16:20

The gospels record a voice from heaven of a Father confirming his ownership of his Son. He was well pleased with him (Mark 1:11). We need God to own what we do!

d. Pray for those who labour

'Brothers pray for us.'

1 Thessalonians 5:25

Make it your business to know who is serving the Lord and where. Pray for the local church workers, for those who travel from church to church with ministry gifts. By praying in this way you begin to pick up the load with them.

e. Pray for open doors

'Pray for us... that God may open a door for our message.'

Colossians 4:3

God uses everything to its fullest advantage. When we pray in this way, not only do we ask God for his help but we live life differently. We begin to look for open doors. We train ourselves in skillfully following the Holy Spirit.

f. Pray for revival

'Sow for yourselves righteousness, reap the fruit of unfailing love and break up your unploughed ground; for it is time to seek the Lord until he comes and showers righteousness on you.'

Hosea 10:12

By revival we don't mean well-attended meetings, but a sovereign move of the Holy Spirit. When revival comes, thousands are swept into God's kingdom. But remember that the greatest hallmark of revival is a willingness in the lives of Christians. *'Your troops will be ready on the day of battle.'* Psalm 110:3

John Wesley, a man who brought thousands to Christ in his lifetime, said, "It seems that God is limited by our prayer life. He can do nothing for humanity unless someone asks him to do it."

If you take some time to study the prayer life of Jesus, you will see that His praying always led him to a point of decision and then to a point of action. Too many Christians pray for God to do something when he is waiting for them to do something. **You cannot pray with sincerity without being moved into your destiny.**

True prayer for revival will get a river going in you!

LESSON 2

Equipped for the Task

True or False

1. T F   We receive faith when the Holy Spirit comes upon us.

2. T F   The key to successful evangelism is learning techniques.

3. T F   The Greek word for 'power' is *dunamis*, which means 'power in action'.

4. T F   God is looking for those who will work with him.

5. T F   Jesus referred to the Holy Spirit as the Comforter; one who comes alongside to give aid.

6. T F   The Holy Spirit is at work only within the church.

7. T F My conscience will either help or hinder me in my life and in evangelism.

8. T F Faith is not enough to ensure success.

9. T F If people don't respond instantly to the message I'm wasting my time.

10.T F I must pray for more power.

Group Discussion

1. Share your experiences of having fellowship with the Holy Spirit.

2. Discuss ways in which you can be co-workers with God.

Personal Assignment

1. Seek this week to have fellowship with the Holy Spirit. Submit every action to him, and learn to listen to his voice.

2. Make a study of Philip's experience in Acts 8:2-40. What lessons about the work of the Holy Spirit can you learn from this encounter?

True of False

1.F 2.F 3.T 4.T 5.T 6.T 7.T 8.T 9.F 10.F

LESSON 3

Always Ready

"If I can talk with one person about Christ and get him to say "Yes" to Jesus Christ - I consider that a very successful meeting." Billy Graham

> *'There is a time for everything, and a season for every activity under heaven.'* **Ecclesiastes 3:1**

We live in a world that has become accustomed to quick answers for long-term problems. World trade deficits in the industrialised nations are massive because people want things now. Ecological problems arise as rain forests are devastated to feed the enormous appetites of industrial giants and levels of personal debt are higher than ever before. Scripture therefore gives good advice when it says:

> *'Do not be conformed to this world - this age, fashioned after and adapted to its external, superficial customs. But be transformed (changed) by the [entire] renewal of your mind - by its new ideals and its new attitude.'*
>
> **Romans 12:2 (Amp)**

1. Natural Progression

We find this worldly attitude creeping into evangelism. Christians often have a quick reaping mentality - they are looking only for instant results. If that is our attitude, we will miss those who are not yet ready for reaping but are ready for sowing.

There is a progression in evangelism - ploughing, sowing, watering, reaping. We need to pray that God will use us in one of these ways in the life of every person we meet. How many encounters did you have with the gospel before you were born again?

Have you ever noticed that everything God does begins with seed? Why did he only create the garden of Eden, why not the world of Eden? When he wanted a people he started with one man - Abraham. Seed is God's secret of success!

In Acts 8:4-8 we read of the enthusiastic response that met Philip as he proclaimed the gospel in Samaria. But could it have been as a result of the sowing Jesus did there, as recorded in John 4:1-42? Philip had the joy of seeing many people brought into God's kingdom:

> *'When the crowds heard Philip and saw the miraculous signs he did, they all paid close attention to what he said. With shrieks, evil spirits came out of many, and many paralytics and cripples were healed. So there was great joy in that city.'*
>
> **Acts 8:6-8**

Philip's proclamation didn't end in Samaria. It continued into Azotus and down into Caesarea (Acts 8:40). But the same dramatic results did not occur. Are you willing to have an Azotus attitude? Are you prepared to be involved at every stage of evangelism? Or does your interest only begin at harvest-time?

It may come as a surprise, but God was at work in you before you were born again. Similarly, other Christians were involved in the harvest before we came along. Some Christians are where they are simply because one or more person prayed for them. Many of us have seen results because others prepared the way:

> *'Others have done the hard work and you have reaped the benefits of their labour.'* **John 4:38**

Your village or town has not only a general history, but a spiritual history. You are just the next link in the chain.

> *'Since we are surrounded by such a great cloud of witnesses let us throw off everything that hinders and the sin that so easily entangles, and let us run with perseverance the race marked out for us.'*
>
> **Hebrews 12:1**

The process of the message is often like this:

- Ploughing
- Sowing
- Watering
- Reaping

No farmer goes out to sow seed in unprepared places. Ground has to be prepared for the seed to be received. In his parable of the sower, Jesus pointed out that seed falling on unprepared ground become food for the birds. (See Matthew 13:4.)

Our natural disadvantage may be that we are not always aware of the ploughed fields, so we rightly sow everywhere. Often we fail to notice where God has already been at work. Oswald Sanders said concerning evangelism, 'Eyes that look are common - eyes that see are rare.'

Much of the ploughing that takes place in people's lives is by God, who prepares the ground for his people to continue the work. As we make contact with an individual, we can explore whether or not this is one of those 'divine appointments'.

Lives can be opened by need, conscience, fear or emptiness.

2. Need

Often life comes to an abrupt halt at the point of crisis:

> *'[The blind man] called out, "Jesus, Son of David, have mercy on me!"... [Jesus] asked him, "What do you want me to do for you?"'*
>
> **Luke 18:38-41**

Life is often busy, filled with many things, and important questions are avoided for as long as possible. When a crisis or tragedy occurs, it has an uncanny way of making people face up to eternity. The compassion that so often captivated Jesus compelled him to respond to deep need and hurt. It should compel us, too:

> *'As God's chosen people, holy and dearly loved, clothe yourselves with compassion.'*
>
> **Colossians 3:12**

We need to be aware of those around us who are at the point of crisis. This often provides the best opportunity for us to help. Sensitive communication can bring healing ointment into sore wounds and often leads to an introduction to your best friend, Jesus. The bereaved family, the divorced single parent, the bankrupt businessman who has lost everything - in their situation they may now realise that they need God. You can be that healing ointment in your community. Don't deal with these people the way the world so often does. Sometimes not knowing what to say, they stay away, or even worse, throw them on the scrapheap of life. God is brilliant at remaking and remodelling, you can be the door through which he starts!

3. Conscience

Today we are often shocked by the apparent lack of remorse in those guilty of serious crimes. Many, however, are weighed down, not by circumstance, but by internal pressure. Guilt is an impossible thing to live with. For some, their dark past haunts them as they try to put a brave face on the future. Others carry guilt not for what they did, but what was done to them. Somehow they feel responsible.

Alcohol and drugs do their worst, not just in their habit-forming destruction, but by anaesthetising the conscience. This pushes into oblivion the voice that says, 'There's something wrong here that needs to be put right.'

> *'God... reconciled us to himself through Christ and gave us the ministry of reconciliation.'*
>
> **2 Corinthians 5:18**

We have a part to play in providing an answer. Too often, Christians see their ministry as prophets of gloom, doom and destruction. Even the Holy Spirit doesn't do that! The Holy Spirit convicts, he never condemns - he reconciles. Condemnation means that the finger of guilt is pointing at you, but that there is no way out. The Holy Spirit, on the other hand, makes you aware of your sin but shows you the road to life.

4. Fear

> *'Men will faint from terror; apprehensive of what is coming on the world.'*
>
> **Luke 21:26**

a. Fear of events

This is usually called worry. Pressures of today's world make for tough living. 'Is my job safe?' 'Is my health good?' 'What will become of my children?'

As a Christian, your biggest attribute ought to be **hope**.

b. Fear of something or someone

People have many fears - spiders, the dark, water, their father. They can be silly fetishes but often they are deep-rooted bondages. They may be the result of bad experiences in childhood. In some cases, though, they can be demonic strongholds.

> *'There is no fear in love. But perfect love drives out fear.'*
>
> **1 John 4:18**

Most people are only too glad to be rid of fears. As Christians, we have the answer to fear. You can help them break free.

c. Fear of God

> *He has...set eternity in the hearts of men.'*
>
> **Ecclesiastes 3:11**

Due to a godly parent or Christian influence, many people are genuine God fearers. They know he exists, and they want to do right. They are already seeking to worship God. But they have to realise not only that God exists, but that he *'rewards those who earnestly seek him.'* Hebrews 11:6.

Help them!

Usually we have to get around preconceived ideas and begin to speak simply and openly. We can do this by challenging them with, 'You may know about God, but do you know him personally?'

Don't dismiss 'religious' people. You'll find many open-hearted Nicodemuses among them. (see John chapter 3).

5. Emptiness

> *'Everyone who drinks this water will be thirsty again but whoever drinks the water I give him will never thirst. Indeed, the water I give him will become in him a spring of water welling up to eternal life.'*
>
> **John 4: 13-14**

At a recent social event, my wife and I sat at a table of professional people. While making introductions and finding opportunity to share our faith, we were amazed to discover that they all confessed to an emptiness and lack of fulfilment in their lives. Many had succeeded with careers and material possessions, but it had left only a void.

Recent books written and studies made of emerging trends tell us that this next century will be hallmarked by great spiritual hunger. These are not just Christians talking - but the world's marketing men (See Megatrends 2000). Someone once pointed out that it isn't so important to know that God reigns, as to know what kind of God reigns. Sometimes we need to grasp the fact that he is sovereign and has placed us where we are, and to expect him to use us there. As the late Arthur Wallis put it, 'The place of God's appointing is the place of God's anointing.' You may be the only light in your dark work place - let it shine!

The days have gone when people lived in walled cities. Our towns and cities may not be built that way now but our lives are. With the escalation of violent crimes, people hurry to and from their places of work, bolting their doors behind them.

The hardest part of personal evangelism is often making the initial contact. Yet every day we meet people in shops, schools, colleges and offices. We all come in contact with people. How about trying the following?

a. Opening Conversations

Talk to people. Thank the waitress for your drink and ask her what kind of day she has had. Sit by someone on the bus rather than on your own. Let your conversation be questions that require more than yes or no answers. Small talk often leads to big issues. Always be thinking that this could be my divine appointment.

If in the event the conversation goes nowhere, don't let your heart sink. At least he or she thinks you are a friendly person.

b. Offering help

Several years ago I found myself crashed on the motorway at six in the morning, having hit some black ice. Unhurt, I scrambled out of an overturned car that lay in the central reservation. Cars passed me on either side, but no-one stopped to help. That may not be an everyday event, but thousands live lives of quiet desparation, ladies often struggle with pushchairs and old folks with shopping. Coming to another's aid can lead to permanent friendships.

c. Asking for help

'Jesus said to [the Samaritan woman], "Will you give me a drink?"'

John 4:7

A neighbour we once had remained closed to all forms of communication until I asked to borrow his ladder. Immediately, he felt safe, he came to my aid and a friendship began.

d. Swimming with the fish!

Jesus was accused of being a friend of publicans and sinners. You, too, can cultivate circles of unsaved friends. They may never come to your meetings, but they may come to your house.

e. Being ready

Becoming a Christian means living a life of adventure. God is a communicating God:

> *'The Spirit told Philip, "Go to that chariot and stay near it."'*
>
> **Acts 8:29**

He obeyed unquestioningly. We need to increase our expectation of God's promptings. They are often small things - making a phone call, sending a birthday card, visiting a neighbour - but they can have a significant effect.

Become like Jesus, who said:

> *'I have called you friends, for everything that I learned from my Father I have made known to you,'*
>
> **John 15:15**

When Jesus was on the cross he declared, 'It is finished', but in one sense he seemed to cut the opening tape and declare, 'It's all just begun'.

LESSON 3

Always Ready

True or False

1. T F The most important part of evangelism is reaping.
2. T F There is a progression in evangelism: ploughing, sowing, watering, reaping,
3. T F God was working here before me. I'm the next part in the process.
4. T F I must wait for people to come to me.
5. T F Compassion should compel us to respond to deep need and hurt.
6. T F It is the place of the Holy Spirit to condemn.
7. T F Religious people are never open to the gospel.
8. T F We need to listen to God's promptings and obey them, even if they are only small things.

Group Discussion

1. Share your experience of divine appointments. Discuss how you handled them.
2. Think of practical ways in which you can increase your circle of acquaintances.

Personal Assignment

1. Before you read any further, make a deliberate point of opening conversations with six people.

True or False

1.F 2.T 3.T 4.F 5.T 5.T 6.F 7.F 8.T

LESSON 4

Sowing the Seed

"Nurture great thoughts, for you will never go further than your thoughts."
Benjamin Disraeli

Ploughed fields don't just stay empty! Cults and sects are often far quicker at sowing their destructive seeds into these areas than Christians are at sowing the truth.

As we will discover in this lesson, there is more than one way of sowing seed. We find Jesus telling us that we are to use both. "Come and see", and "Go and tell". We can sow by:

• Proclamation

• Affirmation

• Demonstration

Very often all three are involved in the process.

1. Proclamation

> *'We proclaim to you what we have seen and heard, so that you also may have fellowship with us. And our fellowship is with the Father and with his Son, Jesus Christ.'*
>
> **1 John 1:3**

Proclamation is using words in order to correctly present the facts. It takes place in different contexts; by individuals, small groups or large crowds. It may be completely spontaneous, as on the day of Pentecost, or deliberately prepared and prayed over.

Words are powerful and effective:

> *'The tongue has the power of life and death.'*
>
> **Proverbs 18:21**

You cannot even become a Christian without confession, for the Bible declares:

> *'It is with your heart that you believe and are justified, and it is with your mouth that you confess and are saved.'*
>
> **Romans 10:10**

Many lives have been destroyed by words, but words can also bring life. As Christians, we have to be careful how we speak, for our own words can help or hinder us.

a. How to use words

E.W. Kenyon said, 'Learn how to use words so they will work for you and be your servants.'

First, get to know God's Word:

> *'The things you have heard me say in the presence of many witnesses entrust to reliable men who will also be qualified to teach others.'*
>
> **2 Timothy 2:2**

In some circles evangelists have a reputation for being "all froth and no substance". A truly successful evangelist will love God's Word, for he knows it to be the sword that the Spirit uses.

> *'Take the helmet of salvation and the sword of the Spirit which is the word of God.'*
>
> **Ephesians 6:17**

Make it your aim to increase your understanding of Scripture. Know how to find your way around the Bible, become familiar with key verses, and know where to find them.

Someone once said. "You should never urge the unsaved man to believe, but you should give him the Word so that he can't help but act on it."

The increase of democracy around the world has led to greater freedom of speech. Witnessing can end up merely as clashes of opinion. We need to use with grace and faith the expression "The Bible says..."

Businessmen adopt spiritual laws and make them work for them. Some even adopt Christian ethics to live by. But it takes a supernatural encounter to produce new birth.

> *'You will know the truth, and truth will set you free.'* **John 8:32**

It's not the truth that sets free - but **knowing** the truth. That's where we come in.

Before new birth can take place, faith has to operate:

> *'Faith comes from hearing the message, and the message is heard through the word of Christ.'*
>
> **Romans 10:17**

The importance of the Word cannot be overstressed. If you are unfamiliar with Scripture, take a look at the following verses. Underline them in your pocket Bible or New Testament and become familiar with where to find them. If possible, memorise at least some of them.

Essential Christian Truth

'Who was Jesus Christ?'	Romans 9:5	'God over all.'
	John 8:58	'Eternal God.'
	Philippians 2:9-11	'Lord.'
'Why did he come?'	John 3:16	'To bring salvation.'
	John 10:10	'To give life in all its fullness.'
'What did he do?'	Matthew 20:28	'Gave his life a ransom for many.'
	1 John 3:8	'Destroyed the devil's work.'

'What about me?'	Romans 3:23	'A sinner.'
	Romans 6:23	'Payment earned will be payment made.'
'What does God require?'	Hebrews 11:6	'Seek him and find life.' 'The Lord requires all to seek him.'
'What must I do?'	Acts 2:38	'Repent, be baptised, receive the gift of the Holy Spirit.'
	Romans 10:9	'Confess Jesus as Lord.'
'Where do I go from here?'	Hebrews 10:25	'Don't give up meeting together.' 'Become part of a church.'
'What if I don't get saved?'	2 Thess. 1:8-9	'End up in everlasting destruction.'

'Be diligent to present yourself approved to God as a workman who does not need to be ashamed, handling accurately the word of truth.'

2 Timothy 2:15 (NASB)

b. Ways of wisdom

'The fruit of the righteous is a tree of life, and he who wins souls is wise.'

Proverbs 11:30

A branch doesn't have to struggle and strive to produce fruit. It is the natural by-product of its life. As we walk in right living with God, we will be fruitful. Many people quote the above Scripture in connection with evangelism. It really means to influence people and win their favour. Wisdom - 'the intelligent application of knowledge' - is required for this to happen.

Personal proclamation requires wisdom. Hitting people over the head with verses, or hiding texts in their sandwich boxes, seldom results in their salvation.

1. Don't be religous!

You need to know the bible but quoting the bible can be perceived as irrelevant - especially if you use an old translation. Sometimes it is better to give your own paraphrase of the principle.

2. Always confer worth on people

Only use your Bible as an offensive weapon against the Devil. With people use it as delightful honey. Some people are pushed away from Christ through the arrogant, offensive behaviour of some Christians. Look for sensible opportunities to sow seed. Remember, we are called to a ministry of reconciliation, not separation. God loves people. No one cares how much you know, until they know how much you care.

3. Learn to stop

A conversation is like a good meal. You know when you've had enough. There are times when we may feel we have to say everything, but learn how to measure spiritual temperatures. Trying to say more than can be accepted at the time may result in a breaking of the relationship. Guard friendships and keep channels open. Try not to allow a valid opportunity to become an argument. Let people have their space.

> *'Don't have anything to do with foolish and stupid arguments, because you know they produce quarrels.'*
>
> **2 Timothy 2:23**

4. Calculate and prepare

Distractions of all kinds are tiresome. Pick your moments. If you are planning to share with your neighbour and you know she is ready, consider arranging for childminders, take your phone off the hook, create and guard opportunities to speak. Make sure that your own kids behave, and do not become a distraction.

5. Be yourself

Use your own language and experiences. Don't exaggerate. On one occasion early in my Christian life, I was asked to give testimony to my salvation. I stood with men who had once been drug dealers. Their stories seemed so colourful, and I felt so inadequate. As my turn approached, I wondered what story I could tell; I tried to think of the most terrible things I had ever done. Then God reminded me that my fate would have been the same as theirs had I not met Christ. I could tell without shame what had happened to me.

'We proclaim to you what we have seen and heard.' **1 John 1:3**

6. Become equal partners

Always make people at ease. Don't patronise and don't be intimidated. Learn to appreciate what God has done in your own life, and be secure.

It is generally better to share with a person of the same sex. Issues of salvation are heart issues, and people often share their most secret longings. Be careful that it doesn't become an opportunity to start up unhealthy relationships.

7. Cultivate good will

Winning souls means having people on your side. You can influence people who may never get saved. They are still used by God in some incredible way to enlarge his work. Where you are able, cultivate good will.

8. Be honest

Sometimes difficult questions come our way. Here are some examples; and perhaps some helpful answers:

Q. 'If there is a God why are there so many wars in the world?'

A. Because God, at creation gave man a free will - together with responsibility for the planet. Man in his greed to take what isn't his starts wars to take what he shouldn't have.

Q. 'Why do so many die in famines or natural disasters?'

A. (i) Some famines are the result of poor government policy - again man's responsibility.

(ii) It is a known fact that there is more than enough food on the planet to feed everyone. But we would rather burn it than ship it, for that would let food prices fall.
(iii) National Religions.
"Righteousness exalts a nation" Proverbs 14:34 If foreign gods are served, are not foreign gods responsible?
History tells us on many occasions that when people turn to God as a nation, divine intervention has changed things.
(iv) Destructive industrialisation is changing the climate around the world.

Q. 'Why do bad things happen to good people?'

A. Sometimes our own fault. (e.g. Driving at speed)
Sometimes its other people's fault (e.g. Pollutants for industrial advance)
Sometimes the devil comes to kill and destroy.
Sometimes it just happens, God is not behind every event.

Q. 'What about other religions?'

A. The Bible says that Jesus is the only way.
Only Jesus died for my sin.
Only Jesus could have died an acceptable death, because only he had no sin of his own.
He was born of a virgin and did not inherit human sin.
All roads do not lead to heaven. Either Jesus is what He claims to be - the way, the truth, the life, or a deceiver. You cannot logically accept Christ's claims and other religions as possible answers.

Q. 'What about people who have never heard the gospel?'

A. God who is a perfect judge will make the right decision. Leave it with him.

Sometimes such questions are genuine. At other times they are red herrings. No sooner have you started to answer one question than another is thrown out. Answer where you can and are allowed to. Don't be afraid to say you don't know but will find out. Consider steering the conversation back to the important issues.

c. The preached word

'I was appointed a preacher:' **1 Timothy 2:7 (NASB)**

Paul spoke of his own calling and declared that he was called to be a preacher, literally a herald or announcer. Earlier in this course, we said that God's covenant provision was principally the person of the Holy Spirit. Equally part of God's covenant provision are the gifts he has given to people. Those people themselves then become gifts to us, enabling us to fulfil the task. God's best gifts are always people. These ministering gifts are also 'God's provision for the vision'.

> *'When [Christ] ascended on high, he led captives in his train and gave gifts to men.'* **Ephesians 4:8**

The preached word is effective:

> *'When the people heard [Peter's message], they were cut to the heart and said to Peter and the other apostles, "Brothers, what shall we do?"'* **Acts 2:37**

Preaching is one method of proclamation clearly ordained by God:

> *'To him who is able to establish you according to my gospel and the preaching of Jesus Christ'.*
> **Romans 16:25 (NASB)**

Even after severe warnings and persecution, the early apostles still felt compelled to continue this process whenever they had opportunity:

> *'They called the apostles in and had them flogged. Then they ordered them not to speak in the name of Jesus, and let them go . . . They never stopped teaching and proclaiming [preaching] the good news that Jesus is the Christ.'*
> **Acts 5:40, 42**

Though we live in a highly visual society, where effective measures of communication can be found in so many ways, sitting under anointed preachers results in salvation. It is in this place that millions of people have found themselves propelled into God's kingdom. All the seed that you have sown can come to harvest at this point. I think that people will tire of decreasing human contact - the preacher's best day is yet to come!

d. Working with the preached word

Personal evangelism is highly effective. But we often fail to maximise our corporate efforts. We need to learn how to make full use of our resources. Here are some factors to consider for evangelistic events, or even just bringing people to church.

1. Plan ahead

Work with your personal contacts towards this event. Warm them up weeks ahead to the idea of coming. Give them a written invitation, making it more definite.

2. Make it easy for them to come

Organise transport or childminders. Arrange to have a meal together before or after the meeting.

3. Play your part

Thoroughly play your part in announcing the event, using posters and delivering leaflets in your street.

4. Believe

Activate your faith. Don't let it freewheel in neutral.

6. Pray

Pray for the unhindered attendance of your friends. Spiritual advance invokes spiritual attacks. Pray for anointing on the preacher and for the liberty of the Holy Spirit.

7. Help your friend relax and be as comfortable as possible

Once your contact is sitting in the meeting, explain what is happening. Don't leave him on his own. Introduce him to someone else if you have to do other things. If an appeal is made, sometimes it is appropriate to say - 'I'll go forward with you if you want.'

8. Lead meetings wisely

If you are responsible for leading these events, consider carefully their purpose:

- Don't introduce songs of adoration or worship. Unsaved people can't enter in, and fail to understand your purpose.
- Sing proclamation songs. Sing the word before it is preached.
- Avoid religious jargon.
- Keep the preliminaries short.
- Keep explaining - tell them what's going on.

9. Follow through your advantage

Don't get discouraged if your friend doesn't respond. Stick with it. He or she may now be one step closer. It is said that it takes six times more fire power for an army to take ground, than to hold ground. Serious effort is required for increase.

10. Explain again

Remember the story of the sower and the soils? (Matthew 13) Jesus told us that if the recipient doesn't understand, then the devil comes and steals the seed away immediately! Don't let him.

2. Affirmation

Being a witness is different to witnessing! An old evangelist said "witness at all times, and sometimes use words." If you are not a witness, witnessing is nothing more than hypocrisy.

> *'You yourselves are our letter written on our hearts, known and read by everybody. You show that you are a letter from Christ'.*
>
> **2 Corinthians 3:2-3**

Many homes have Bibles, but few are read. Your life, however, is very often read from cover to cover. You become the written record on feet. Your life interprets the message. As Oswald Sanders once said. 'Example is far more powerful than precept.'

Often the values we take for granted are alien to the world. As a result, we stand out like lighthouses.

> *'Do everything without complaining or arguing, so that you may become blameless and pure, children of God without fault in a crooked and depraved generation, in which you shine like stars in the universe as you hold out the word of life.'*
>
> **Philippians 2:14-16**

a.The hope factor

> *'We have this hope as an anchor to the soul firm and secure.'*
>
> **Hebrews 6:19**

Many people are set adrift because they have no anchor of hope. Misshapes such as anti-depressants or compulsive spending are used in an effort to fill the void. We seldom have to say we have hope, for it is a very visible quality, totally affecting the way we live.

The Greek word for hope *(elpis)* means 'the happy anticipation of good'. To know that God is both for you and with you must make you an optimist. Often that is in complete contrast to the non-Christian's outlook.We should also be prepared to speak about it:

> *'In your hearts set apart Christ as Lord. Always be prepared to give an account to everyone who asks you to give the reason for the hope that you have.'*
>
> **1 Peter 3:15**

Have you looked in the mirror recently? Does your face smile - or frown? Have you listened to your own words? Are they words of faith - or unbelief?

Depressed Christians are a bad advertisement for the overflowing life of God. If you are like that, see your pastor or a counsellor and get help. Remember, it's not what people say they believe - it's what they say that people hear.

b. Other contrasting qualities

1. Righteousness

Live out your faith. Righteousness is best seen outworked in your life. Speaking about it gives the impression of being self-righteous or pompous. Your time-keeping, your honesty, even the kind of calendar on your office wall, can speak volumes.

2. Language

Make sure your language is not only good and wholesome, but positive and without complaint.

3. Attitude

Watch your attitude, particularly towards authority. Are you grateful or do you feel hard done by?

4. Good works

> *'Live such good lives among the pagans that, though they accuse you of doing wrong, they may see your good deeds and glorify God on the day he visits us.'*
>
> **1 Peter 2 :12**

c. Be prepared to speak

A different lifestyle without an explanation can be ineffective.

On visiting the church in response to an advertisement, Anne gladly gave her life to Christ. Jayne, a member of the church, came forward to greet her. I later learned that these two worked together. Anne had observed a difference in Jayne, but had never been given an explanation. To Anne, Jayne was just a nice lady. Perhaps if Jayne had spoken up, Anne would have come to

Christ earlier. Are there Annes sitting in your workplace?

3. Demonstration

> *'I labour, struggling with all [Christ's] energy, which so powerfully works in me.'*
>
> **Colossians 1:29**

> *'There are different kinds of working, but the same God works all of them in all men.'*
>
> **1 Corinthians 12:6**

The word translated 'energy' and 'working' in these verses comes from the same Greek root word which literally implies the outward working of energy. Paul was saying that the power at work in him was outworking from him.

> *'These signs will accompany [follow] those who have believed.'*
>
> **Mark 16:17 (NASB)**

Many Christians follow meetings where they expect the supernatural, but the Bible promises that miraculous signs will follow them.

a. Why demonstration?

Jesus promises:

> *'[You] will do even greater things than these.'*
>
> **John 14:12**

On several occasions I have seen supernatural healings take place with unsaved people present. Contrary to the popular myth, 'If I see a miracle then I'll believe,' the sceptics present walked away as sceptical as ever, choosing to accept coincidence as the most plausible explanation. Healings and miracles are not there to make people believe, for the source of saving faith is always God's Word. However, signs and wonders do have a way of attracting attention, often pointing people towards the living Christ.

b. Your kingdom come

> *'How can anyone enter a strong man's house and carry off his possessions unless he first ties up the strongman? Then he can rob his house.'*
>
> **Matthew 12:29**

Demonstration in sign and wonder, by healing or miracle, is proof of the fact that God's kingdom has invaded the space-time world of humankind. Jesus said:

> *'If I drive out demons by the finger of God, then the kingdom of God has come to you.'*
>
> **Luke 11:20**

Jesus came not only to provide salvation in the shape of eternal life in a place hereafter, but to bring the power of the age to come into the here and now! The power of King Jesus' government has impacted us here.
John said:

> *'The reason the Son of God appeared was to destroy the devil's work.'*
>
> **1 John 3:8**

The cross was not a sad event or a fatal mistake, but an awesome judgement brought to bear on Satan:

> *'Having disarmed the powers and authorities, he made a public spectacle of them, triumphing over them by the cross.'*
>
> **Colossians 2:15**

The proof carried through supernatural manifestations is not that God exists but that he is Lord. We are called to be witnesses of the resurrection. The same Jesus who worked wonders then is working them now.

c. Charisma

Signs and wonders can take place through: miracles (for example, John 2:1-11), words of knowledge (John 4:18); healing (John 5:8-9), and deliverance (Matthew 9:32-33).

In 1 Corinthians 12 we read of spiritual gifts that become available to us through the Holy Spirit. One Greek word for 'gift' is *charisma*, from which we get the word 'charismatic'. It specifically means 'gift of grace', a gift involving grace on the part of God as the donor. Paul said:

> *'Eagerly desire the greater gifts.'* **1 Corinthians 12:31**

Which are the greater gifts? The greatest gift is the one that has the greatest impact at that moment in time. While there is a distribution of gifts within a context of a meeting, it would be wrong to think, 'I have the gift of healing and she has the gift of prophecy.' The gift you have is the Holy Spirit - and he has all the gifts.

'Desire' in the above verse literally means 'lust after'. This kind of longing produces results. We should therefore 'lust after' spiritual gifts that we may see them operate through us. Mentally centering everything on meetings can hinder us. Spiritual gifts are for life; they have their greatest impact out in the world.

d. How to pray for sick people

Within the sphere of evangelism, healing is often the most necessary gift. Never be afraid to pray for sick people. You don't have to be in a special meeting; we frequently pray for sick people in homes. Only on one occasion has a person refused when I've offered to pray for them after explaining that I believe God could heal them. Here are some points you may find helpful:

1. Have true faith

Know without doubt that it is God's will to heal. God is not the author of sickness. Faith can be blown away when the words 'if it be your will' are added.

> *'As you go, preach this message: "The kingdom of heaven is near". Heal the sick, raise the dead, cleanse those who have leprosy, drive out demons. Freely you have received, freely give.'*
> **Matthew 10:7-8**

> *'The punishment that brought us peace was upon him, and by his wounds we <u>are</u> healed.'*
> **Isaiah 53:5**

> *"By his wounds you <u>have</u> been healed."* **1 Peter 2:4**

2. Be at peace yourself

Never pray out of pressure or guilt. According to Romans 14:23, what is not of faith is sin.

3. Never put the person under pressure

Explain to him what you are doing, help him relax and give him scriptural reasons.

4. Don't be in a hurry

On one occasion Jesus had to pray twice for a man who first saw people as trees walking around (Mark 8:22-25).

5. Listen to the Holy Spirit

Call for his help as you pray. He may just show you the way to pray on that occasion. Do a study of the variety of ways in which Jesus prayed. Sometimes there may be issues of unforgiveness or sin that need confessing first.

6. Don't project on to the person your lack of faith

Some people are locked up for years because they have been blamed for failure.

7. Help the person believe

Keep pointing him or her towards the Lord. Sometimes posture helps a person receive - for example, reaching out hands in faith.

8. Speak with authority to the sickness

Command it to leave and healing to come, in Jesus' name. Then pray for God to heal.

9. Lay hands on people

When you lay on hands, a transmission of life takes place:

- Blessing is imparted.
- The Holy Spirit is imparted.
- Authority is imparted.
- Healing is imparted.

When you lay hands on people:

- Don't push, be gentle.
- Don't press down.
- Don't have bad breath (use mints if necessary).
- Don't have dirty or sweaty hands.
- Don't put your hands where they shouldn't be (dignity and respect).
- Place your hands only when you are aware that this is the moment of breakthrough.

e. Overcoming culture

On one occasion Paul questioned the Corinthians:

> *'Are you not acting like mere men?'*
>
> **1 Corinthians 3:3**

Although this was referring to carnality and sin, it is equally carnal to attempt to serve God merely with human resources.

Western culture has seemed resistant to the supernatural. Sadly, in many Christian circles, there is an anti-supernatural stand. There are foolish people who think they know better than God. Materialism accounts for much of this humanistic level of living.

Instead of accepting this aspect of culture, let us live by faith, believing for better things.

That great missionary William Carey said *"You should believe for great things from God, and attempt great things for him."*

....

LESSON 4

Sowing the Seed

True or False

I. T F Proclamation is the only effective means of evangelism.

2. T F It is important for me to become familiar with Scripture and to use it wisely in winning souls.

3. T F It is essential to present the whole gospel to a person at one sitting.

4. T F The preached word is still effective today.

5. T F In one sense, we are God's written record on feet.

6. T F Healings and miracles demonstrate that God's kingdom has invaded the space-time world of humankind.

7. T F. The greatest spiritual gift is the one that has the greatest impact at that moment in time.

8. T F The Bible's promises concerning miraculous signs are confined to our church meetings.

Group Discussion

1. Discuss your experiences and lessons learnt in operating in the spiritual gifts.
2. Discuss the concept of unity. What do you understand by it?

Personal Assignment

1. The best way of getting started in anything is often to observe someone who is doing better than average in that area. Think of someone you know who prays for sick people and ask him to let you pray with him.
2. Examine your personal testimony at work, home, etc. Does your life affirm or deny the gospel? Highlight areas for improvement.
3. Familiarise yourself with the scriptures in this lesson concerning Jesus. Make it your goal this week to mark these in your pocket Bible and to memorise three of them.

True or False

1.F 2.T 3.F 4.T 5.T 6.T 7.T 8.F

LESSON 5

Getting Fruit that Lasts

"If faith dies success will fold its wings." E W Kenyon

There must come a point in the lives of all who respond to the gospel when they know they have been converted. For some, it is at their first encounter. Others may need several encounters. We should not be in a desperate hurry but fully prepared to be patient. Yet there comes a point when a decision needs to be made:

> *'When the people heard [the message], they were cut to the heart and said to Peter and the other apostles, "Brothers, what shall we do?"'* **Acts 2:37**

If every person within a fifty-strong church brought one person every year into this experience, and each convert did the same, by the seventh year the church would consist of over three thousand people! Can you believe for that one person this year?

In this lesson we will consider how to bring someone into this experience.

Clarity is vitally important. Bringing someone to Christ does not mean getting them merely to make a decision. There are many people living under the impression that 'theirs is the kingdom of heaven' because, in a meeting at some time, they signed the appropriate decision card, raised their hand or prayed in response to an appeal.

Clearly, while such action may be involved in their experience, it is only a means to an end, not the end itself. There is only one state worse than a man who is not born again - it is the man who believes he is, but isn't.

1. Don't Auction Salvation

In our presentation of the gospel we have no right to conceal the true cost of discipleship. Jesus Christ takes no prisoners. He calls all who would follow him to die! It is the end of the old life and the beginning of the new. They must lose their independence and identify with his community, the church:

> *'Anyone who does not take up his cross and follow me is not worthy of me. Whoever finds his life will lose it, and whoever loses his life for my sake will find it'*
>
> **Matthew 10:38-39**

Sometimes we lose sight of what the true benefits are. They include:

- A life restored into relationship with God.
- An acquittal from our guilt.
- Eternal life.

> *'Praise the Lord, O my soul, and forget not all his benefits - who forgives all your sins and heals all your diseases, who redeems your life from the pit and crowns you with love and compassion.'*
>
> **Psalm 103:2-4**

- The new possibility that almighty God is for you, not against you.
- The finding of purpose and meaning for your existence.
- An open door to God's resource for life.

The Bible is full of head counts in response to the proclaiming of God's Word. Numbers do matter, for they represent real, living people. Today, however, people are often considered saved because they showed interest, prayed or put up their hand. It is better to treat everyone initially as enquirers, not converts. This ensures that they are diligently helped.

2. What Must Happen?

Complete salvation comes to the complete man or woman from a complete response. Man is a tripartite being - spirit, soul and body. The presentation of the gospel must touch each of these areas.

When these areas have been touched, what is produced within the person will be:

a. Accountability

He stops blaming his upbringing. 'It isn't the social worker's fault or the government's policies - it's me!'

> *'If we claim we have not sinned, we make him out to be a liar and his word has no place in our lives.'*
>
> **1 John 1:10**

b. Acceptance

He no longer attempts to work it out for himself but accepts God's way of salvation:

> *'If [we are saved] by grace, then it is no longer by works; if it were, grace would no longer be grace.'* **Romans 11:6**

c. Access

He hands over the keys to every area of his life, allowing God to clean up each room:

> *'Search me, O God, and know my heart; test me and know my anxious thoughts.'* **Psalm 139:23**

He will begin to think "How does this new life affect my....

- Marriage?

- Business?
- Work?
- Relationships?"

3. Kingdom and Church

Sometimes we find it much easier to speak about meetings, events, buildings and church than about God, Christ, sin and salvation. So, we need to be careful. These other things may come into our conversation - for they are part of our experience, and it is an appropriate approach to say "come and see." But our relationship with Jesus Christ ought to be the main talking-point. It is presenting the King of the kingdom:

> *'By faith in the name of Jesus, this man whom you see and know was made strong.'*
>
> **Acts 3:16**

> *'With great power the apostles continued to testify to the resurrection of the Lord Jesus.'*
>
> **Acts 4:33**

While our faith may be exercised to see our local church grow, our first priority is to advance God's kingdom. There is a difference! The kingdom is God's rule. The church is God's family, and a vehicle through whom the kingdom comes. We aren't only out to spread the church but to enlarge the kingdom - to see people from every tribe and nation submitting to God's rule. We are called to be salt in society (Matthew 5:13), and that means influencing beyond the church.

Jesus said, *'I will build my church, and the gates of Hades will not overcome it'* (Matthew 16:18). We proclaim the good news of God's kingdom, introducing them to its King, and Jesus commits himself to building the church.

Having the correct vision will prevent us being parochial. We will show the same interest in everyone, not just in those whom we hope to see added to our church. People are then brought to birth on the right basis. Many will then be added to your church, but some will be added in other places.

4. Understanding Terms

Christians frequently use jargon that they have acquired and have not thought through. If you ask an unchurched person if they have been "Washed in the blood of the lamb" they will think you're insane. How many of us have said to a person, 'Invite Jesus into your heart'? Some argue that this is inaccurate, for it is Jesus who receives us, our lives being placed in him.

> *'If anyone is in Christ, he is a new creation; the old has gone the new has come!'*
>
> **2 Corinthians 5:17**

> *'God made him who had no sin to be sin for us, so that in him we might become the righteousness of God.'*
>
> **2 Corinthians 5:21**

It is important to understand that, by placing your life in Christ, you were:

- In him when crucified (Galatians 2:20).
- In him when buried (Romans 6:3).
- In him when raised (Romans 6:4).

I have always found the simple bible story of Noah to be a great aid in explaining this. Like Noah we are placed into an ark - Jesus. We then sail through judgement and land in a new world, called abundant life.

Back to the Future

Not only are you placed in Christ past, you are placed in Christ future! You have already faced the judgement that is to come:

> *'Instruction about baptisms, the laying on of hands, the resurrection of the dead, and* ***eternal judgement.'***
>
> **Hebrews 6:2**

No wonder you find peace when you find Christ

5. Leading Someone to Christ

There are three steps a person needs to take in response to the gospel. Don't stop short; as much as you are able, help him or her to take them all:

- Repentance and belief
- Baptism in water
- Baptism in the Holy Spirit

> *'Repent and be baptised, every one of you, in the name of Jesus Christ for the forgiveness of your sins. And you will receive the gift of the Holy Spirit.'*
>
> **Acts 2;38**

a. Repentance

Repentance means "a change of mind that leads to a change of direction". People have to change their minds about themselves and about God. A child once said repentance means "when you are sorry enough to stop".

You can help people by offering to pray with them. Most people (not only the early disciples) don't know how to pray, but their willing involvement is essential. Don't force them to say what is not meant or what is unreal to them. It can sometimes be helpful to get them to pray after you, line by line. Their prayer should include:

- Regret, sorrow.
- Renouncing of sin.
- Reaching for forgiveness.
- A plea to God for his acceptance.
- Receiving with thanks his forgiveness and accepting the new life he gives.

Pray for them. If appropriate lay your hands on them, seeing them released from the devil's strongholds.

Repentance isn't a negative, but a positive. It lets go of one direction and embraces another. Faith is activated towards God, committing the new Christian to stand on God's Word, accept God's answer and embrace God's life.

b. Baptism

When Jesus gave his followers the command to make disciples, he also commanded them to 'baptise'. Baptism isn't an optional extra; it is a command (Acts 2:38). The only valid baptism is believer's baptism, for repentance and faith must come first. But note that it is believer's baptism, not adult baptism. Believing children should be baptised, too.

Our only example of an evangelist shows Philip at work. In both recorded accounts of conversion through his ministry he saw the basic necessity of baptism:

> *'When they believed Philip as he preached the good news of the kingdom of God and the name of Jesus Christ, they were baptised, both men and women.'*
>
> **Acts 8:12**

> *'He gave orders to stop the chariot. Then both Philip and the eunuch went down into the water and Philip baptised him.'*
>
> **Acts 8:38**

For many people, life before becoming a Christian was a story of sin, hurt and regret. Water baptism is the point at which the door to the old life is closed.

Water baptism is not only a drama demonstrating inward salvation. It is most importantly an essential foundation. Leading someone to Christ equally means leading them through the waters of baptism. In doing so, the proper foundation is laid in their lives:

'We were... buried with him through baptism into death.'

Romans 6:4

Baptism is more than a ceremony. When appropriated by faith, it actually does something. It cuts off the past, and cleanses the person's conscience from sin:

'This water symbolises baptism that now saves you... not the removal of dirt from the body but the pledge of a good conscience towards God.'

1 Peter 3:21

- Ensure that new converts are baptised as soon as possible. New Testament converts didn't wait until the next annual baptism.
- No mandate is given in the bible that Christians have to be baptised by church officers. Tradition in some places has it that way.
- The Bible not only sees water baptism as a witness to the world, but is a very important personal issue for a personal encounter to lay a personal foundation.
- All scriptural examples show that a person can't baptise himself.
- At their baptism, people are baptised both into Christ and into his body, the church:

'Go and make disciples of all nations, baptising them in the name of the Father and of the Son and of the Holy Spirit.'

Matthew 28:19

Q. Is any method of baptism valid?

A. No, the only New Testament method was by full immersion.

Q. Does it have to be in a particular place?

A. No. Rivers were commonly used in the New Testament. Do it in the most convenient place, where there is enough room to get the whole person under, and where others can watch if they want to. If your church building doesn't have a baptistry, try a swimming pool.

Q. Can anyone do the baptising?

A. There is no clear direction given in Scripture. I would only suggest that it needs to be a person who is born again.

Q. What do we say over them?

A. Baptise them according to their own confession into either 'the name of the Father and of the Son and of the Holy Spirit' or simply 'into Jesus', as he is God incarnate. Matthew 28:18 Acts 10:48

Q. What if they were baptised by immersion before being born again?

A. Baptise them again. Repentance and faith must come first.

Q. What if they claim to have sinned since their first water baptism and need to be dipped again?

A. There is no need to do it again. After repentance, once is enough. They must appropriate by faith the initial act.

c. Baptism in the Holy Spirit

Baptism in the Holy Spirit isn't for the select few. For powerful, effective Christian living, it is essential that new Christians are plugged into power. Acts gives five accounts of people receiving the Holy Spirit (Acts 2:4; 8:17; 9:17; 10:44-46; 19:6). On three of these occasions Christians who had already received the Holy Spirit prayed for others to receive - 'Go and do likewise.'

In Acts 10:44-46 Peter knew that the people had received the Holy Spirit when they spoke in tongues. You should expect the same. Even that would be settling for less, according to Acts 19:6, for they prophesied as well! Look for a supernatural manifestation of the Holy Spirit.

Here are some keys to helping people through into this experience:

- Build faith by showing its basis in Scripture. (Acts 15:1-35).
- Build faith by showing people that they are included. (Acts 2:38-39).
- Assure them that God will hear their praying. (Luke 11:13).
- Confirm that they are clear about the issue, with no hidden sin problem. He is a Holy Spirit.
- Explain about tongues - not a learnt language but God-given. Explain its purpose (1 Corinthians 14:4). It is not for a select few but for all (1 Corinthians 14:5).
- Explain that they speak with Holy Spirit enablement (Acts 2:4). God will not manipulate their tongue.
- Explain that the Holy Spirit is gentle by his nature, and will not force himself on them. The demon possesses, the Spirit impresses.
- Be at peace.
- Get them to pray first, giving thanks with expectation.
- Lay hands on them and pray for them.

d. Confession

It is not possible to be born again without saying so:

> *'If you confess with your mouth. "Jesus is Lord," and believe in your heart that God raised him from the dead, you will be saved. For it is with your heart that you believe and are justified, and it is with your mouth that you confess and are saved.'*
>
> **Romans 10:9-10**

Confession means 'declare openly' or 'speak freely'. This kind of confession is the result of deep-seated conviction. James declares that the tongue is the hardest part of the body to tame:

> *'No man can tame the tongue. It is a restless evil, full of deadly poison.'*
> **James 3:8**

When the tongue is yielded to the lordship of Christ, it is a sure sign that the rest has yielded. Open confession needs to be made constantly and consistently. If you fail to instruct new Christians in the importance of this, you are leaving them short of God's measuring line. Help them find courage to tell friends and family. Promise to pray for them.

6. Clear in Our Objectives

What are we after? What do we want to achieve? Evangelism ought not to be a lifestyle of dead works. If you view this as a chore rather than a calling for which God will equip you, you can expect disappointment. Rather:

> *'Do you not know that in a race all the runners run, but only one gets the prize? Run in such a way as to get the prize.'*
> **1 Corinthians 9:24**

a. Clarify your mission

Don't be afraid of facing up to reality. Knowing where you are is the only way to plot your course for where you are going. Have you been clear in the goal you have for new birth? Are you effective? Does your approach need to change? Do you need different results? If you keep doing the same thing you'll get the same results. Only a fool will do the same thing expecting different results.

Does your approach to people need to change? The purpose of evangelism is not to make a stand for the faith. There is a time and place to nail your colours to the mast concerning truth, but here the purpose is to win people.

b. Clarify your message

The focus of our message is Jesus Christ. Traditionally, evangelism has been addressed to individuals, and has been exclusively concerned with the forgiveness of sins. Yet the gospels set evangelism in the context of the inauguration of the kingdom (rule) of God:

> *'From that time on Jesus began to preach, "Repent, for the kingdom of heaven is near."'*
>
> **Matthew 4:17**

> *'Seek first his kingdom and his righteousness, and all these things will be given to you as well.'*
>
> **Matthew 6:33**

Contrary to a title once given to a book, Satan is not alive and well on planet earth. Jesus our victor has inflicted on him serious wounds and will soon bring him down with the final death blow.

c. Clarify your methods

People are motivated to learn only to the degree that the subject matter is seen as essential. They don't take much notice of fire escape route notices behind hotel doors. But in the event of a blaze they could be crushed in the rush! Frequent travellers do not listen to the air steward as he conveys emergency procedures, but a sudden bang gets everyone looking.

We must contextualise the message to our generation. We are a multi-racial, multi-cultural community. We must learn the skill that Jesus had in being able to touch all kinds and classes. Like Paul, we can become *'all things to all men so that by all possible means I might save some.'* 1 Corinthians 9:22.

> *'[I pray] that the participation in and sharing of your faith may produce and promote full recognition and appreciation and understanding and precise knowledge of every good [thing] that is ours in [our identification with] Christ Jesus - and unto [his glory].'*
>
> **Philemon 6 (Amp)**

If you are intending to work with ethnic groups, get to know them and try to understand their culture.

Maybe your methods need to include giving people space! In a recently acquired traditional church building, we were about to remove all the pews. We decided to leave some, so that the 'not so confident' could sit at the back and have some space if necessary.

The main thing, is to keep the main thing, the main thing!

....

LESSON 5

Getting fruit that lasts

True or False

I. T F Salvation means the end of the old life and the beginning of the new.

2. T F Salvation is available to the person who simply makes an intellectual decision to follow Christ.

3. T F We aren't out to spread the church but to enlarge God's kingdom.

4. T F The Bible tells us to invite Jesus into our hearts.

5. T F Repentance simply means saying sorry.

6. T F Baptism should be considered for a future occasion.

7. T F Baptism in the Holy Spirit is for everyone, not just those in certain kinds of local church.

8. T F It isn't possible to be born again without declaring it openly.

9. T F Evangelism can be merely a way of nailing our colours to the mast concerning truth.

Group Discussion

I. Play-act leading someone through to Christ

2. What would you do after leading him or her to personal salvation?

Personal Assignment

Consider how best you would explain the basic truth to:

- An eighty-year-old lady who has been to church all her life.
- A Hindu who believes that all religions lead to God.

True or False

1.T 2.F 3.T 4.F 5.F 6.F 7.T 8.T 9.F

LESSON 6

The Next Generation

"The succesful leader is a man who has learnt that no failure need be final."
O. Sanders

1. Look Again

What are the outer limits of evangelism? The instruction of the New Covenant was not to make new converts, but to make disciples. The process of evangelism doesn't end until you see your children's children brought through. That is the goal we have in mind - seeing not only the joy of new birth, but also the living, mature love for God that you have imparted being reproduced again.

The purpose of this lesson is to underscore the importance, now that we are being successful, of discipling our new converts.

2. Legoland Christianity

Wouldn't it be so convenient if God produced 'Legoland' Christians? They would fit so easily into our programmes; their smooth, perfectly-fitting characters clicking nicely into place. Instead, God in his creativity hews out living stones. He is looking for those who will work with him in shaping them up.

With the pressures of modern day society we find greater openness to the good news of Jesus than ever before. It is important that those who were yesterday's babies in Christ become today's fathers, mothers and brothers to those newly born. We will need all the help we can get.

3. Daily Contact

In developing those early disciples, Jesus lived, ate and walked with them. He was there to answer their awkward questions and address their attitudes.

He was there to explain patiently when truth seemed to miss them by a million miles. He was there to defend them when the religious leaders threw accusations at them. When faith seemed to fail, and tough times came, he prayed for them:

> *'Simon, Simon, Satan has asked to sift you as wheat. But I have prayed for you, Simon, that your faith may not fail. And when you have turned back strengthen your brothers.'*
>
> **Luke 22:31-32**

Someone once asked, 'Is there life after meetings?' With widespread conversion in mind, we must see that there is life for new believers especially. It isn't enough to leave them to float for a week until the next meeting or new converts' class. These spiritual babies need daily attention. Build up a friendship that involves, at least, a regular contact by phone.

4. Responsible Parents

God wants us to be responsible parents to those he has entrusted to our care. These people need answers to the problems they will face at work on Monday. They need to know how they should react to the non-Christian members of their family. Above all, they need a friend who will stand with them in crisis, as the debris of their old life is pulled away.

As we make this way of living a matter of course, quality friendships will give rise to quality Christians. The added bonus is, that not only do they become part of a new family, but we become part of theirs. This results in new relationships, with new opportunities to share our life, love and experiences.

5. Prowling Predators

> *'When trouble or persecution comes because of the word, he quickly fails away.'*
>
> **Matthew 13:21**

Each time God's Word is planted in a person's life, the enemy will come to shake it out. Jesus told the parable of the sower to open our eyes to what is happening. You can be sure that some effort will be made to shake out the Word. Remember, though:

> *'The weapons we fight with are not the weapons of the world. On the contrary they have divine power to demolish strongholds.'*
>
> **2 Corinthians 10:4**

We have a responsibility to pray and care, watering the seed that has been sown.

> *'Be self-controlled and alert. Your enemy the devil prowls around like a roaring lion looking for someone to devour. Resist him, standing firm in the faith.'*
>
> **1 Peter 5:8-9**

6. Mentor Them

Many of us enjoy the blessing of godly leadership. We are to submit not only to the leaders but also to one another (Ephesians 5:21). We must assume a care and concern for each other. We are our brother's keeper (see Genesis 4:9).

> *'The goal of our instruction is love from a pure heart and a good conscience and a sincere faith.'*
>
> **1 Timothy 1:5 (NASB)**

All the meetings we attend and the teaching we receive are, according to Paul, for a purpose: our lives are to change. When discipling new Christians, the following attributes ought to be your goal.

a. Pure-hearted love

'Pure heart' as used in 1 Timothy 1:5 means 'cleansed heart'. In his Sermon on the Mount, Jesus said, 'Blessed are the pure in heart' (Matthew 5:8). This means not only cleansed but purified, resulting in an unalloyed, unmixed heart. Light and dark are in stark contrast. Conversion involves a process of changing value systems. Some of these contrasting values include:

Kingdom of God	Worldly
Give	Get
Serve	Assert
Confess	Cover up
Forgive	Retaliate
Love never fails	Love cools
Search the Scriptures	Check the stars
Total righteousness	Shady dealings
Utter honesty	White lies

Love from a pure heart will also mean love for your brothers:

> *'We know that we have passed from death to life, because we love our brothers.'* **1 John 3:14**

Such love results in new Christians wanting to be a part of the local community of believers. We need to help them forge relationships and feel at home. Sometimes we need to recognise the different levels of commitment in church life expressed in the diagram below, and our aim should always be to take people further in, to a deeper level of commitment.

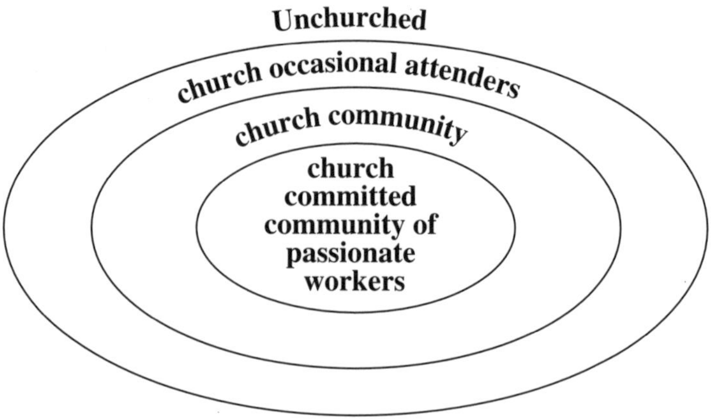

b. Good conscience

The world has lost all sense of shame and boundary. Anything now goes. Frequently, people's lives are intertwined with immoral issues, or their lifestyles are contrary to Scripture. Many are held by habits of drink or drugs, or are snared by financial problems. Being brought into the congregation of the righteous can be quite a shock!

While no-one advocates wrong living, God often handles one issue at a time in their lives. On one occasion I remember a streetwise biker coming to the Lord. With chains, leathers and helmet he strolled into his first meeting. A concerned older lady, unaccustomed to such sights in her church, confronted the young man immediately. 'This isn't the way to dress here,' she told him. The following week he came with a new tuxedo, bow tie and fancy shirt. Somehow this didn't satisfy her either, even though the man genuinely did his best.

Let us not be too quick to pass judgement, or to allow a person's appearance to colour our thinking about them.

c. The grace factor

Concerning Jesus, John tells us:

> *'We have seen his glory, the glory of the One and Only, who came from the Father; full of grace and truth.'*
>
> **John 1:14**

> *'From the fulness of his grace we have all received one blessing after another.'*
>
> **John 1:16**

Very often we forget our early experiences of salvation - how we felt, the mood swings, the times of despondency, the great heights of excitement. Since we have been filled with some grace, we need to know how to measure that towards others added more recently.

'But grow in the grace and knowledge of our Lord and Saviour Jesus Christ.'

2 Peter 3:18

It is interesting that this is growing not just in grace, but in the grace of Christ. The Greek word for grace (*charis*) means 'bestow delight and favourable regard'. It is a friendly disposition from which kindly acts proceed. It will be outworked through patience, gentleness and faith.

New Christians will not become mature overnight; a discipling process must take place. Here are some pointers to working this through:

1. See them regularly

A close relationship is important.

2. Ensure that the relationship is both natural and spiritual

It is easy to go to extremes - becoming engrossed in spiritual issues without finding each other, or being so natural that it becomes hard to approach the Bible, pray together or speak into issues.

3. Maintain integrity

Never get closely involved on your own with someone of the opposite sex. If a friendship starts with someone of the opposite sex, make sure your partner or another person from your church is fully involved.

4. Pray together

First, let them see you pray, verbally, simply and naturally. Then get them to pray with you. Soon they will feel comfortable to pray on their own.

5. Help them read the Bible

Give some explanation of the Bible's structure. Help them to get started, then check their progress.

6. Help them worship

Teach them to enjoy God's presence with thankfulness.

7. Help them identify God's voice

Help them to know when God is speaking into their lives - that Bible verse that seemed to jump out, or that song in the meeting or the testimony they identified with. Show them God's awareness of their situation.

8. Never separate them from their families

As they change, help them to be a witness in their home and among their family.

9. Begin instructing them on God's standards

Show them God's plan for Christian marriage, his attitudes towards their studies or their job, etc.

10. Don't tackle too much at a time

Look for the point at which their conscience is stirred, and help them from there.

11. Be available

12. Don't be afraid to speak into their lives

Remember, when we speak into the lives of other Christians we should do it with grace and love.

13. Pray, and promise to pray for them

14. Help them find other relationships

15. Instruct them on how they can be effective in evangelism

16. Be practical

17. Help them to get integrated into the local church.

18. Teach them how to serve, preferably by your own example
It is pointless merely to teach spiritual truths when they are struggling to feed or clothe their families. Show them practical love.

All the above ideas are basic, but they have to be grasped to enable strong, solid growth to take place.

d. Sincere faith

As J.I.Packer wrote, 'The only proof of past conversion is present convertedness.'

Our goal should be to build sincere faith into new Christians. Due to life's circumstances, false faith is soon exposed and real faith stands for what it is. There are key elements in a faith life, however, and we need to sow them into new converts that they, too, may produce them. These include:

1. Faith's source

Faith's source is always Scripture. Encourage young Christians to stand on it. Don't build into people a dependence on you. Make sure that you are secure enough for healthy relationships without emotional bondages. By warmth, love and example, build them into God. Remember hurt people hurt people - keep yourself healthy! Even if you encounter major challenges, consider carefully who you should share these with. It's possibly better for you to share with your mentor or another mature Christian. Your words and attitudes could seriously affect this young converts life!

2. Ruling their thinking

> *'We take captive every thought to make it obedient to Christ'*
> **2 Corinthians 10:5**

3. Sound words

We have already spoken about the key role that words play in our salvation. They are also active in our well-being and in our walk of faith.

4. Perseverance

Believe and keep on believing. Don't project 'unreal faith' on to people, leaving them in a place where they feel failures if they aren't up to the grade. Sound faith has its feet on the ground but its eyes on God.

e. Signs of health to look for

1. Changed lifestyle

2. Developing friendship with God

New Christians should be hearing God and seeing answers to prayer, and the Bible should be coming alive to them.

3. Joyful and open confession to being a Christian

If confession is missing, check it out!

4. Fitted into the body

That doesn't necessarily mean immediately an 'official member' of a church, but they have a supply of life - friendships with other Christians.

5. Beginning to serve

It isn't only your church; it is theirs, too.

6. Taking part in meetings

7. A growing understanding of God's purposes

7. Good Communication

Most of us never fall short on intention. But the practical outworking is always a challenge. Satan tries his best to stop new believers playing their part. He goes by many names in the Bible, including 'the accuser of our brothers' (Revelation 12:10). Use these keys to help new Christians live for God:

- You have two ears and one mouth. Use them in that proportion - twice as much listening as talking.
- Tackle the issue, not the person. Remember, we have a ministry of reconciliation.
- Try to understand before pressing to be understood.
- Don't be afraid of confrontation, but handle it with grace.
- Be a peacemaker, not merely a peacekeeper (see Matthew 5:9). Anything to keep the peace always ends up in separated people. To be a peacemaker demands courage and the willingness to see things through. It will mean discussion, dialogue and humility.
- Understand well the importance of maintaining correct relationship as outlined in Matthew 5:23-24 and Matthew 18:15-16.

8. Digging In

The building in which you are sitting has a foundation. You can't see it, but it is used every day of the building's life. Without it, subsidence and collapse soon take their toll.

Spiritually, you have a foundation, too.

Consider Jesus' words about the wise man and the foolish man (Matthew 7:24-27). What hallmarked the difference between the two? Not that they heard the Word but rather that the wise man acted on the Word. The foundations laid when a person is converted have to be built upon.

When discipling new Christians, it isn't so much a case of moving on to deeper things, but moving IN to the same foundation. Unlike a building, you don't so much build on your Christian foundations as build into them. Take time to dig them in well; make sure they are understood:

a. Repentance

Repentance means a change of mind. If it becomes a foundation, it is something permanent and always there. It means a permanent change of direction; there is no going back. Whatever question life throws at the person, he has already decided to choose God's way:

> *'Flee from all this [false teaching], and pursue righteousness, godliness, faith, love, endurance and gentleness.'*
>
> **1 Timothy 6:11**

b. Faith

Hebrews 6:1 speaks not only of faith on its own, but of faith in God. This means living a life of faith, relying on him always. New Christians will only be able to live in peace when they understand the full significance of what God has done for them. They now know that they are accepted before him. Life will test their faith, not only when they depend on him on their day of salvation but when they continue to do so.

c. Water baptism

While new Christians have the experience of water baptism just once, each day they must build on it,

1. It becomes their number one weapon against sin

> *'All of us who were baptised into Christ Jesus were baptised in to his death... in the same way count yourselves dead to sin but alive to God in Christ Jesus.'*
>
> **Romans 6:3, 11**

When faced with temptation, they should bring back to memory their baptism and see themselves dead!

2. It helps them experience freedom from accusation

Satan certainly is 'the accuser of our brothers'. For many people, life before conversion was a life of shameful activity. Peter says:

> *'This water symbolises baptism that now saves you... not the removal of dirt from the body but the pledge of a good conscience towards God.'*
>
> **1 Peter 3:21**

3. It helps them embrace the cross

Water baptism is not only the dying to wrongs but also the dying to rights. Jesus Christ is Lord yesterday, today and tomorrow.

d. Baptism in the Spirit

> *'If the Spirit of him who raised Jesus from the dead is living in you, he who raised Christ from the dead will also give life to your mortal bodies through his Spirit who lives in you.'*
>
> **Romans 8:11**

This resurrection power gives life even to a person's natural body to live the new way.

An initial experience will fill people, but they need to be continually filled. The power then received helps the new Christian to:

- Pray (Romans 8:26)
- Witness (Acts 1:8)
- Produce fruit (Galatians 5:22-23)
- Exercise spiritual gifts (1 Corinthians 12:4-11)
- Deal with and overcome sin (Romans 8:13)

e. Added

The measuring-line in the book of Acts is 'the Lord added to their number' (Acts 2:47). Evangelism doesn't end with the first step. It is an ongoing process which has built into itself the ongoing ability to reproduce.
As someone once put it, 'New converts are born - but disciples are made!'

....

LESSON 6

The Next Generation

True or False

I. T F We can leave new Christians to God's care.

2. T F God wants us to be responsible parents to new Christians he has entrusted to our care.

3. T F Satan will try to shake out the Word planted in a person's life.

4, T F The goal of discipling is to increase intellectual knowledge.

5. T F We need to show new Christians love from a pure heart.

6. T F Repentance means simply saying I'm sorry.

7. T F The new Christian experiences water baptism just once, but must then build on it each day.

8. T F Baptism in the Holy Spirit happens just once without a need for further filling.

Group Discussion

I. Discuss ways in which you could integrate new Christians into the church.

2. Discuss together the foundational principle of repentance. Share areas where you have had to decide to go God's way. What have been the benefits of doing that?

Personal Assignment

1 .Study the concepts of repentance. water baptism and baptism in the Holy Spirit. How have they become foundational in your life?

2. Think back to your conversion. What did people do that helped you grow? What hindered you? How would that affect you in discipling others?

True or False

1.F 2.T 3.T 4.F 5.T 6.F 7.T 8.F

LESSON 7

Get UP and GO

"Obstacles in the pathway of the weak become the stepping stones of the strong." Thomas Carlyle

The Star Wars movies are not only fun to watch, nor do they just tell the story of a conflict between the forces of good and evil, but they also tell the tale of how a young, self-seeking space pirate is enrolled to help the cause. Han Solo, a futuristic bounty hunter is persuaded to join the crusade and make a difference. We also need to join up and get to the point of committing ourselves to succesful fruit production. Let's not just live for ourselves but live for God and his purposes.

> *'Thanks be to God, who always leads us in triumphal procession in Christ and through us spreads everywhere the fragrance of the knowledge of him.'*
>
> **2 Corinthians 2:14**

> *'Stand firm ... with the belt of truth buckled round your waist, with the breastplate of righteousness in place, and with your feet fitted with the readiness that comes from the gospel of peace.'*
>
> **Ephesians 6:14-15**

It is interesting how God's concepts differ so much from ours: his understanding of standing firm is not to stand still. Anyone dressed for battle, prepared and with the proper boots on, has got some marching to do. You, however, need to stand firm on the inside, while advancing on the outside. The Christian who caves in within dies without!

1. Standing Firm

a. Dealing with rejection

The biggest single bullet that appears to shoot down advancing troops is rejection or the fear of rejection. The ego takes a severe battering, courage ebbs and confidence blows away.

1. The CURE of the cross

Contrary to popular belief, the cross is not your allocated burden in your life. It is not the load you must carry but a means of execution. It is the death blow to the self life.

Dead men don't have an ego and feel no blows. Living from this place makes you immune to these kinds of bullets. Paul said:

> *'May I never boast except in the cross of our Lord Jesus Christ, through which the world has been crucified to me, and I to the world.'*
>
> **Galatians 6:14**

The way of effective evangelism is the way of the cross. We must die to inhibiting factors like tiredness, Monday morning blues or shyness. G.E Ladd once said, 'The cross is not a burden but an instrument of death.'

The New Testament word for 'witness' is *martus*, from which we get our word martyr. It means one who bears witness by his death. We may never physically have to die for our faith like so many have, but we will only bear witness by total death to self.

> *'Preach the Word; be prepared in season and out of season; correct, rebuke and encourage - with great patience and careful instruction.'*
>
> **2 Timothy 4:2**

Are you prepared:

- To give your time?
- To give your money?
- To share your faith when it isn't convenient?
- To lose your privacy and independence?

> *'I tell you the truth, unless a grain of wheat falls to the ground and dies, it remains only a single seed. But if it dies, it produces many seeds.'*
>
> **John 12:24**

Biologically, the life in a seed doesn't die but changes form. The seed has all the potential, but until its hard shell is broken open and germination takes place, it's life is locked up. The cross brings us to that place of brokenness for openness.

Jesus is our example:

> *'Let us fix our eyes on Jesus, the author and perfecter of our faith, who for the joy set before him endured the cross, scorning its shame, and sat down at the right hand of the throne of God.'*
>
> **Hebrews 12:2**

Die to your embarrassment and the fear of what others think of you. Within the natural seasons, spring comes after winter. So, too, in God's economy, life comes from death.

2. Mirror mentality

> *'Anyone who listens to the word but does not do what it says is like a man who looks at his face in a mirror and, after looking at himself, goes away and immediately forgets what he looks like.'*
>
> **James 1:23-24**

Look into the mirror of God's Word and develop a new identity - the one God gives:

'More than conquerors.'	Romans 8:37
'Righteousness of God.'	2 Corinthians 5:21
'As bold as a lion.'	Proverbs 28:1

3. Pray for boldness and wisdom

See Acts 4:31, James 1:5.

4. Shake off the dust

> *'If anyone will not welcome you or listen to your words shake the dust off your feet when you leave.'*
>
> **Matthew 10:14**

In evangelism, we are caught up with life or death issues. We aren't offering a hobby or interest. Christianity isn't some club that people can join. Consequently, there are times when the offer of life brings venomous reaction.

I remember on one occasion being deeply hurt by a particularly arrogant response I received on a doorstep. I walked away grieved in spirit. At those times you are truly grateful for a Comforter alongside. The above scripture came to mind, and with a deliberate action I shook myself free from that encounter, leaving that man's response with him. My action had a liberating effect. I could carry on without being accountable for his reaction. After all, there were others who would listen.

b. Dealing with other fears

> *'You will know the truth and the truth will set you free.'*
>
> **John 8:32**

Sometimes fear comes through not knowing! Jesus promises that his truth will bring liberty. Live in the Word, and let the Word live in you.
You can also be assured that God's perfect love liberates:

> *'There is no fear in love - dread does not exist; but full-grown (complete, perfect) love turns fear out of doors and expels every trace of terror!'*
>
> **1 John 4:18 (Amp)**

Past failures sometimes haunt us. Yet no failure need be final. Learn from your mistakes, pick yourself up and get going. Failure doesn't need to finish you, but quitting will!

2. Anointing

a. Secret of success

In the Old Testament, when a priest or king was separated for holy service, he was anointed with oil. Oil signifies the presence of the Holy Spirit. It is his activity, movement and blessing that brings life:

> *'The yoke will be destroyed because of the anointing oil.'*
>
> **Isaiah 10:27 (RAV)**

b. Ever remaining

> *'As for you, the anointing you received from [the Holy One] remains in you.'*
>
> **1 John 2:27**

c. Unlocked by agreement

Read Psalm 133. You are convinced, I hope, of the necessity of body ministry. We are all members of one body, the church, with different parts to play. In almost all of Paul's letters he made a plea to the churches:

> *'Be of one mind.'* **2 Corinthians 13:11**

'I appeal to you...that you may be perfectly united in mind and thought'

I Corinthians 1:10

God's idea of unity is often different from ours. We usually emphasise the negative: if we haven't disagreed, then we must be together. God's idea of unity is a unity of purpose - a communion of faith, vision and effort.

With events involving the whole church, your active involvement is essential for success. The scriptural concept of unity carries with it the idea of being of the same planting, grafted together, resulting in a joint life. Your inaction will affect the rest.

The invitation of Jesus is:

'Take my yoke upon you and learn from me, for I am gentle and humble in heart, and you will find rest for your souls. For my yoke is easy and my burden is light.'

Matthew 11:29-30

We need to know a yoking to the task. When we are harnessed to Christ and to each other, the task becomes light. Once yoked, God can play his part:

'I planted the seed, Apollos watered it, but God made it grow'

1 Corinthians 3:6

According to Psalm 133 there appears to be a place where God bestows blessing - it is where he finds unity. Covenant living invokes the anointing of God.

As high priest, Aaron found himself saturated with anointing oil. It flowed from his head to his beard and down his royal robes. The oil set him apart as priest. He then administered the life and salvation of God to his people. David compares the unity of brothers to that. Where God finds common life, common faith and common purpose, walked out in righteousness, blessing is the outcome.

3. Whatever is in Your Hands

God's usual method of blessing concerns what you already have or are doing:

- Moses' staff became the tool for unlocking mighty miracles. Exodus 4:2-5.
- The little boy with five loaves and two fish provided the basis for an awesome supply. (John 6:8-13).

> *'May the favour of the Lord our God rest upon us; establish the work of our hands for us.'*
>
> **Psalm 90:17**

Begin where you are! Use whatever is at your disposal and expect God to bless. Remember, for you as a Christian, it is written:

> *'Whatever he does prospers.'*
>
> **Psalm 1:3**

This thing works!

4. Be Prepared

It is good to live in expectation. It may be helpful to gather material for your preparation:

- Own a pocket Bible or New Testament. Familiarise yourself with useful scriptures.
- Have copies of the New Testament or gospels available to give to new Christians. Have some good literature on hand to give away. It needs to be clear, concise and contain the full gospel. (My own booklet, *This is for You!* Reapers Trust, 1994, is ideal for those seeking the truth about God.)
- Have a calling card or personal tract, with an address where you can be contacted.

5. By All Means

Affirmative evangelism should be your way of life. Wise living will influence the people you meet every day. But why not consider initiating your own proclamative plans? Consider:

a. Door visitation

Go with a friend. Ask God to direct you to where you will find ploughed fields ready for sowing. Go with real expectation. Most people will be closed, but go looking for that one in a particular area who could be the key to releasing others.

b.Open-airs

Open-air meetings were powerfully used by the early church and can be powerful today, too. To be successful, they need to be well prepared. Use drama, sketchboard and good testimony. Keep a fast-moving programme that attracts attention. Train other Christians to work as a team in these events. Learn how to:

- Form a crowd.
- Initiate speaking to someone as he or she moves away.
- Avoid distracting people from listening to the testimony or watching the drama.
- Choose the right songs. Use powerful songs that carry the message in their words, proclaiming Christ's lordship, the power of his name, the changing influence of his Word.

c. Wider friendships

Increase your circle of acquaintances. Talk to people in your area through low-key social events that serve to build bridges. Always make a habit of inviting someone with you to church each week.

6. End-time Heralds

As we have seen, the old Greek evangelist ran with the news of the general's victory. His message confirmed not only the triumph - but that the king himself was coming. We are approaching the countdown to the coming of our King. This time, he will not come to a hidden corner of the globe. Instead, every eye will see him. Before his coming an acceleration of messengers will be seen announcing victory and freedom, enjoying the harvest that they reap. While so many Christians, particularly in the West, are waiting for another move of God, thousands of others are realising that the move God has already made in sending the Holy Spirit was more than enough; they already have what it takes. They are changed lives, changing lives.

Jesus told us to lift up our eyes and see the harvest fields (John 4:35). The harvest is ripe - but are the reapers ready? Will you be one of them?

....

Lesson 7

Marching Orders

True or False

I. T F Standing firm as mentioned in Ephesians 6 means to take stock without actually doing anything.

2. T F The way of effective evangelism is the way of the cross.

3. T F We need to look in the mirror of God's Word and find our true identity.

4. T F Living in God's love drives fear out of our lives.

5. T F God's anointing ebbs and flows.

6. T F Anointing can be released through covenant living.

7. T F God will bless whatever is in our hands as we use it for him.

Group Discussion

1. How have you coped with rebuffs? What helped you get going again?
2. Make a plan of something that you could do together - then put it into action.
3. Plan a door visitation of your street. Prepare a small event, such as a video, in your home so that you can invite them to something.

Personal Assignment

1. Draw together useful tools such as literature and pocket Bibles.

2. Produce a small personal tract, containing your testimony, that you can give away.

True or False

1.F 2.T 3.T 4.T 5.F 6.T 7.T